TERRORIST DOSSIERS

U.S. COUNTERSTRIKE

American COUNTERTERRORISM

Samuel M. KATZ

Lerner Publications Company/Minneapolis

This book is dedicated to those brave Americans who have
sacrificed their lives so that others may live in freedom.
SMK

Publisher's Note: The information in this book was current at the time of publication. However, the
publisher is aware that news involving current events dates quickly. Please refer to the websites on
page 69 for places to go to obtain up-to-date information.

Lerner Publications Company
A division of Lerner Publishing Group
241 First Avenue North
Minneapolis, MN 55401 U.S.A.

Website address: www.lernerbooks.com

Library of Congress Cataloging-in-Publication Data

Katz, Samuel M., 1963–
     U.S. counterstrike : American counterterrorism / by Samuel M. Katz.
        p.   cm. — (Terrorist dossiers)
     Summary: Examines the origins, tools, techniques, and major operations of the following United
States counterterrorism forces: Delta Force, Navy SEALs, CIA, FBI, and Department of Homeland
Security.
     Includes bibliographical references (p.) and index.
     ISBN: 0–8225–1569–5 (lib. bdg. : alk. paper)
     1. Terrorism—United States—Prevention—Juvenile literature. 2. Terrorism—Prevention—
Government policy—United States—Juvenile literature. 3. National security—United States—
Juvenile literature. 4. Police—Special weapons and tactics units. [1. Terrorism—Prevention.
2. National security.] I. Title: United States counterstrike. II. Title: American counterterrorism.
III. Series: Terrorist dossiers.
HV6432.K38 2005
363.32'0973—dc22
                                             2003020992

Manufactured in the United States of America
1 2 3 4 5 6 – DP – 10 09 08 07 06 05

CONTENTS

Army Rangers: one of the oldest U.S. special forces units, with roots before the American Revolution. The Rangers consist of land, sea, and airborne units that can be quickly deployed for a variety of tasks, including to provide backup to Delta and other U.S. forces.

Army Special Forces: also unofficially called the Green Berets. This unit is made up of highly trained commandos prepared to undertake unconventional warfare, reconnaissance (information gathering), direct action (raids and assaults), and counterterrorist missions.

Charles Beckwith: the original commander of Delta Force

Osama bin Laden: founder and commander of al-Qaeda. Bin Laden was among the mujahideen (Islamic warriors) supported by the CIA during the Soviet war in Afghanistan (1979-1989).

Central Intelligence Agency (CIA): a federal agency charged with collecting and evaluating foreign intelligence and counterintelligence critical to U.S. security. The CIA has also carried out covert and counterterrorist operations.

commando: a member of a military unit that is especially designed for special operations, such as undercover work and raids behind enemy lines

Delta Force: the most highly trained and top secret special force in the U.S. military. Delta was unofficially formed in 1977 as part of the U.S. Army. Delta's mission is specifically counterterrorist in nature.

Department of Homeland Security: a federal department formed in 2002 to coordinate security information and to prevent, combat, and respond to terrorism against the United States and its people

Diplomatic Security Service (DSS): a law enforcement agency within the U.S. Department of State. The primary duty of the DSS is to protect U.S. government officials around the world. Many DSS officers are posted to embassies.

William "Wild Bill" Donovan: founder of the Office of Strategic Services (OSS)

Federal Bureau of Investigation (FBI): a division of the U.S. Department of Justice, the FBI is responsible for investigating federal crimes. Since September 11, 2001, the FBI has also played a growing role in counterterrorism.

Hezbollah: a Shiite terrorist group based in Lebanon. Hezbollah seeks an Islamic government in Lebanon and has attacked U.S. sites in the Middle East.

Saddam Hussein: the former president of Iraq. Hussein was accused by the United States of having weapons of mass destruction and of possibly supporting international terrorism. He was deposed by a U.S.-led war that was launched against Iraq in March 2003.

the Middle East: a geographical and political term that usually refers to nations in eastern North Africa and southwestern Asia

Navy SEALs: a part of the Naval Special Warfare Command (NAVSPECWARCOM). These sea, air, and land teams have specialized skills that make them uniquely qualified for hostage rescues and other counterterrorist operations. SEAL Team SIX is dedicated to counterterrorism.

New York Police Department Emergency Service Unit (ESU):
New York City's law enforcement's main special
operations branch. The ESU is trained and equipped to
handle extreme emergency situations of all kinds,
including terrorist attacks.

Office of Strategic Services (OSS): the forerunner of
the CIA. The OSS was established during World War II to
gather intelligence about the enemy and to conduct
undercover operations behind enemy lines.

operator: a member of Delta Force. While most
counterterrorism forces are called operatives, Delta
prefers the term "operator."

paramilitary: a term describing a force that is built on
a military model but is not necessarily part of the
official military

al-Qaeda: an Islamic fundamentalist terrorist group
founded and commanded by Osama bin Laden. Al-Qaeda was
behind the attacks of September 11, 2001.

security classifications: levels of security applied to
government information. The primary three levels are
confidential, secret, and top secret. Each member of a
counterterrorist team is assigned security clearance at
one of these levels.

special operations: military or other government-directed
actions that are carried out by specially trained groups
but that do not fall under the category of conventional
combat or warfare. Spying, hostage rescues, and
undercover raids, especially during peacetime, are
generally considered special operations.

Special Operations Group (SOG): The CIA's highly covert special operations arm. The SOG was modernized and expanded in the late 1990s and has since taken an active role in a wide variety of counterterrorism activities.

SWAT team: standing for Special Weapons and Tactics, SWAT teams are specialized units of local law enforcement. Team members are trained to respond to especially dangerous or difficult situations including terrorism.

Taliban: a very strict Islamic fundamentalist government that held power in Afghanistan from 1996 to 2001 and that supported and protected Osama bin Laden and al-Qaeda

Task Force 121: a specialized unit formed to hunt and capture high-profile targets such as Osama bin Laden and Saddam Hussein. The force combines elements of many U.S. counterterrorism, military, and intelligence groups. Task Force 121 took part in the December 2003 raid that captured Hussein.

tradecraft: the techniques and methods of unconventional warfare, espionage, or other elements of special forces and counterterrorism work

the West: a geographic and political term that usually refers to the United States and Europe

INTRODUCTION

In keeping with the hijackers' demands, the pilot had parked the airliner far from the tarmac's runway lights. The terrorists had commandeered the U.S. jet in the skies over the Middle East and had claimed to have wired the plane with explosives. They would not hesitate to detonate them, the terrorists promised, if anyone challenged or resisted them. They had already executed two hostages and had threatened to begin killing one more every ten minutes until their demands—the release of imprisoned comrades—were met. The deadline for the executions to begin was swiftly approaching. The passengers were terrified and exhausted.

At the other end of the airstrip, far from the view of the news cameras that had gathered at the scene, fifty Americans were assembled around a diagram of the jet. Dressed in black fatigues and carrying night-vision goggles and a wide array of weapons, they listened attentively to the assault briefing. The operation was routine. The unit had trained for just such a situation time and again. All that was left was to work out last-minute glitches and to incorporate the latest intelligence into the final plans. One thing was certain: the aircraft could not be allowed to take off. The ordeal would end here.

Finally, the moment came. Moving under the cloak of darkness, the assault force stealthily approached the aircraft and took up positions around it. Snipers armed with high-powered weapons ringed the plane. At 3:55 A.M., the signal was given. With weapons at the ready, commandos climbed onto the jet's wings and crept toward the door. At 3:58 they blew the doors open, simultaneously cutting off power to the airliner and plummeting the cabin into pitch-black darkness. The team's night-vision goggles turned the dark into light, but the hijackers were blind. As the hostages screamed, the panicking terrorists became easy prey for the commandos streaming into the aircraft. One by one, each terrorist was shot dead with three bursts of gunfire—one to the head and

U.S. counterterrorist forces train vigilantly to carry out their important duties.

two to the chest. Meanwhile, the rescue force urged the passengers to remain in their seats amid the chaos. "WE ARE AMERICANS," a voice shouted into a megaphone. "PLEASE STAY DOWN!"

This mission never happened in real life. It was a training scenario—one of dozens conducted by the U.S. counterterrorist community each year. But while the setup is make-believe, the purpose of these training sessions is deadly serious. They help to prepare some of the most highly skilled operatives in the world for one of the most important jobs: keeping the United States and its people safe from terrorism, wherever it might strike.

FIRST STRIKES:
EARLY U.S. COUNTERTERRORISM

Seeptember 11. The words alone summon unforgettable images and powerful emotions. On that day in 2001, two hijacked airliners crashed into the twin towers of the World Trade Center in New York City. A third plunged into the Pentagon near Washington, D.C., and another—almost certainly intended for a fourth target such as the White House—crash-landed in a Pennsylvania field. Close to three thousand people were killed, making the terrorist strike the largest ever to take place in U.S. territory.

The attacks on September 11 brought new attention to terrorism—and the need for counterterrorism—in the United States.

These attacks changed the face of terrorism—and of U.S. counterterrorism—forever. In fact, many Americans think that the nation's counterterrorism program was formed largely in response to that horror. However, counterterrorist groups had been in place long before that fateful day.

Three tiers of U.S. forces are responsible for battling the underground armies of terrorism. One level, primarily military, executes direct action and hostage-rescue operations against terrorists around the globe. Another level gathers intelligence on terrorist forces. Finally, a broad third tier is made up of law enforcement units inside the United States, from federal agents to city cops. Together these groups address an enormous and critical task: keeping the United States safe from those who seek to replicate the events of September 11.

Modern counterterrorism groups have their roots in tactics and special operations forces used as long ago as the American Revolution (1775–1783) and the U.S. Civil War (1861–1865). More official groups were formalized as subsets of the armed forces during World War II (1939–1945). They soon proved highly valuable in conducting reconnaissance and sabotage missions behind enemy lines, as well as engaging in more traditional fighting.

Another important development was the formation of the Office of Strategic Services (OSS) in 1942. This agency, separate from the military, took charge of such areas as undercover missions and intelligence gathering behind enemy lines during the war. The OSS became an indispensable resource, creating a new understanding of the importance of covert intelligence and its collection.

Following World War II, the special operations community slowly continued to develop but still remained in the background. However, by the time President John F. Kennedy took office in 1961, new threats had emerged. Communism—a political and economic theory based on the idea of communal, rather than private, property—was taking hold in many nations in Asia and Eastern Europe. Most Communist nations sought not only to reform themselves but also to install Communist systems in other countries—by force, if necessary. The democratic United States, with an economy based on individual property and free markets, grew increasingly suspicious of Communism's spread. The resulting tension was known as the Cold War. It brought the United States and the large Communist nation of the Soviet Union into conflict many times during the last half of the twentieth century, although outright war never resulted.

Kennedy believed that conventional, traditional tactics could not win the Cold War. He advocated a new focus on developing special forces, which could be used to fight Communist power and other challenges or dangers throughout the world. Kennedy saw these forces as made up of specially trained, uniquely motivated professional soldiers. For his support and development of these groups—particularly of the Army

President John F. Kennedy speaks with an officer of the Green Berets.

Special Forces, nicknamed the Green Berets—Kennedy is remembered by modern special forces members as a leader and benefactor.

In conflicts including the Vietnam War (1954–1975), some special forces would develop bad reputations as undisciplined troublemakers. This negative publicity affected both support and funding for the groups. But they survived, remaining among the military's most dedicated members.

| THE ADVENT OF TERROR |

Originally, counterterrorism was not the primary concern of these elite battalions. But that's not to say that terrorism did not exist. In fact, it had been a troubling international issue for years. The United States had dealt with several attacks, most emanating from the Caribbean and Central America, where many people deeply resented U.S. involvement and influence in the region. Some local rebel groups struck out at U.S. interests with violent terrorist strikes.

The most virulent terror campaign at the time, however, was directed against Israel. Founded in 1948 in the former British-held territory of Palestine, this Jewish nation had struggled with terrorism from the outset. An Arab-Israeli war that same year created thousands of Palestinian refugees. Groups emerged pledging to create a Palestinian homeland out of Israel, and some turned to terrorism as a tactic. The problem was not yet global, nor a major issue in the United States.

However, as Palestinian attacks against Israeli citizens and interests grew more public and more extensive, they garnered international attention. In 1968 members of the terrorist group the Popular Front for the Liberation of Palestine (PFLP) hijacked an Israeli plane. The PFLP held the passengers hostage for weeks before the ordeal finally ended. Subsequent incidents included the notorious Skyjack Sunday in 1970, a highly orchestrated attack in which PFLP operatives hijacked four planes on the same day.

While these attacks aroused widespread awareness and concern, the international fight against terror truly began in 1972. In September of that year, Palestinian terrorists carried out a brutal attack against Israeli athletes competing in the Summer Olympics in Munich, West Germany. The West German attempt to save the Israeli captives failed miserably, and all eleven hostages and one policeman were dead by the time five of

West German police, dressed like athletes and carrying submachine guns, climb down from the roof of the building where the Israeli hostages were seized. Tragically, the rescue attempt failed.

the eight terrorists themselves were killed. While U.S. citizens were not the focus of the attack, called the Munich Olympic Massacre, the horrifying incident was highly publicized. Israel's tragedy made clear the need for highly trained counterterrorist forces, and hostage-rescue operations became a top priority around the world.

Throughout the rest of the 1970s and into the 1980s, terrorists continued to strike through bombings, hijackings, and hostage takings. The terror hit home for Americans in November 1979, when a group of Islamic militants attacked the U.S. embassy in Tehran, Iran. A mob of students and Revolutionary Guards (special forces organized to protect the Islamic state) seized the building, taking the people inside hostage.

■ ■

Crisis in Iran

Tehran, the Islamic Republic of Iran. *November 4, 1979. The U.S. Marine Corps Security Guards (or MSGs, as they are casually known) were guarding the embassy. They could practically feel the tension crackling in the air. Anti-American hatred had been building in Iran like steam gathering force inside a pressure cooker. The tensions had existed long before an Islamic revolution had ousted the pro-American shah (Iranian ruler) some ten*

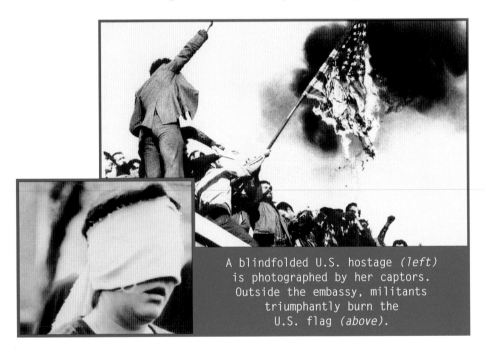

A blindfolded U.S. hostage *(left)* is photographed by her captors. Outside the embassy, militants triumphantly burn the U.S. flag *(above)*.

months ago and had replaced him with the charismatic cleric Ayatollah Khomeini. After the revolution had taken place, Americans no longer felt safe inside the city. The U.S. embassy itself was surrounded by rifle-toting Revolutionary Guards who openly called for the destruction of the "Evil Empire" of the United States.

In such a volatile atmosphere, the marines weren't about to risk being caught off guard. They had a detailed plan of action, in case any organized assault on the embassy should erupt. All classified material would be burned, and the embassy staff would seek shelter inside secured rooms. The marines, armed with assault rifles and shotguns, would be left to fight any intruders who gained entrance to the embassy.

Yet even the best-laid plans—and even the most fortified embassy and most dedicated guards—are virtually helpless in the face of a mob's rage. On that day, approximately three thousand Iranian students and Revolutionary Guards poured over the embassy walls and onto the grounds, spurred on by radio propaganda and religious fervor. The marines could do little to stop them. If they fought back, they would almost surely be overpowered and killed. What would happen then to those inside the embassy, whom they were there to protect? Capture by the mob, with at least the slim hope of a commando rescue or a diplomatic compromise, offered a better chance than certain death. By the end of the day, more than fifty U.S. hostages were in the hands of the Revolutionary Guards. (They would remain so until their release in January 1981.)

A U.S. Marine stands guard outside the bombed U.S. embassy in Beirut.

Terrorist attacks intensified dramatically in 1983, when the Islamic terrorist group Hezbollah, based in Lebanon, began an onslaught against U.S. and Western targets in the Middle East. On April 18, 1983, a truck bombing of the U.S. embassy in Beirut, Lebanon, killed 63 people. Six months later, on October 23, 1983, Hezbollah agents bombed the U.S. Marine barracks in Beirut, killing 241 U.S. servicepeople and wounding more than 100 others. Yet another attack followed on December 12, 1983, when Hezbollah terrorists bombed the U.S. embassy in Kuwait.

| **STRIKING BACK** | Beset by domestic terrorist emergencies, countries such as Israel, Great Britain, and Germany had already begun to respond. Counterterrorism was unlike conventional warfare. The key to defeating terrorists lay in unrelenting firepower and innovative tactics. Counterterrorist units had to think and operate like terrorists. These units had to be cunning, stealthy, preemptive, and unforgiving in battle.

The United States joined these global counterterrorism efforts. However, much of that effort was absolutely covert, with forces operating deep in the shadows. The U.S. military's specialized groups, which included

CHARGIN' CHARLIE

Charles Beckwith was born in Atlanta, Georgia, in 1929. Turning down a chance to play professional football with the Green Bay Packers, Beckwith joined the U.S. Army and was an early volunteer for its special forces. In 1963 Beckwith became one of the first U.S. Army officers to study the British 22 Special Air Service Regiment (SAS) in action.

Beckwith's SAS experience would come in handy when he was sent to Vietnam in 1965. In a 1966 rescue operation, Beckwith was shot in the stomach with a 12.7mm machine gun. Critically wounded and nearly declared dead by army surgeons, Beckwith recovered and continued his service in the military. He even went back to Vietnam—a return to duty that earned him the nickname of Chargin' Charlie. That same determination and fearlessness came into play when Beckwith was charged with commanding Delta Force. Beckwith was determined to ensure that this brand-new counterterrorist unit achieved the highest standards of intelligence, quick thinking, and unflinching action in the face of danger.

"Chargin' Charlie" Beckwith

Beyond the military, the efforts of the Central Intelligence Agency (CIA), which by 1947 had evolved from the OSS, provided important counterterrorist work. CIA spies and analysts gathered foreign intelligence and studied the data so that it could be evaluated, shared with Beckwith's Delta and other counterterrorist units, and acted upon. ■

the Navy SEALs and the Army Special Forces, were tasked with rescuing hostages and targeting terrorists. The army's Delta Force, led by Charles Beckwith, was dedicated exclusively to counterterrorism and was prepared to travel thousands of miles at a moment's notice to respond to an attack.

■ ■

Kidnapped

In the terrorism world, *Imad Mughniyah was as ambitious— and as arrogant—as they came. As Hezbollah's special operations commander, he was a cold-hearted killer. He was also a calculating master in the deadly match of terrorism versus counterterrorism.*

On April 18, 1983, Mughniyah watched the departure of the driver he had dispatched to blow up the U.S. embassy in Beirut, Lebanon. This attack, the first of Hezbollah's suicide truck bombings, was designed to achieve more than the deaths of a few dozen U.S. citizens. The embassy held nearly every

IMAD FAYEZ MUGNIYAH

A "Most Wanted" poster for Imad Mughniyah warns that he is armed and dangerous.

U.S. intelligence agent assigned to Lebanon. Mughniyah knew that by hitting the embassy he would be wiping out U.S. intelligence assets in the country. Mughniyah was successful. Among the sixty-three dead was Kenneth Haas, a top-ranking CIA official at the embassy.

But Mughniyah was not finished. On March 16, 1984, Hezbollah agents kidnapped William Buckley, Haas's replacement, as he drove to work with a packet of classified materials handcuffed to his wrist. Buckley was a human treasure trove of top secret information, and his captors were determined to extract all CIA classified material from their prisoner—even if it meant torture. More than one year later, Buckley died in captivity Meanwhile, Mughniyah remains at large.

■ ■

As the CIA battled its own challenges, other agencies at the federal level also joined in fighting terrorism. The Diplomatic Security Service (DSS) managed internal security and the protection of U.S. officials, wherever they might be. Meanwhile, the federal government's law enforcement branch, the Federal Bureau of Investigation (FBI), developed a team to handle hostage situations. Finally, while often overlooked in favor of more glamorous groups, one of the most critical counterterrorist weapons became local law enforcement.

| A NEW ERA | September 11 brought the U.S. counterterrorist community largely out of the shadows. Many people realized for the first time that the United States was vulnerable to lethal and well-coordinated attacks by its enemies. The counterterrorism community itself saw that if the United States were to defeat well-funded, determined terrorist groups such as al-Qaeda, it could not simply deploy its forces in response to terrorism. It had to go on the offensive, anywhere and everywhere that terrorists posed a danger to national security. To organize information better and to focus U.S. efforts more closely on counterterrorism, a whole new federal department—the Department of Homeland Security—was created.

Propaganda posters, such as this one praising bin Laden and September 11, highlight the international terrorist threat to the United States.

Although much of its activity is still highly confidential, the national counterterrorist community has emerged to fight a new war against a dangerous new enemy. U.S. forces are in Iraq, Afghanistan, and throughout the Middle East, as well as in Southeast Asia, Africa, and Europe. Together, they fight the global War on Terror every day.

ARMED AGAINST TERROR:
U.S. MILITARY
SPECIAL FORCES

Each of the Department of Defense's many branches plays a role in the counterterrorism fight.

At the forefront of U.S. counterterrorism is the military, which is responsible for direct action against terrorists. The military's ability to act effectively—by deploying soldiers either to preemptively terminate a terrorist or to quickly react to an attack—is critical. The nation's military, in turn, supports other agencies' global effort to battle terrorists. While the military has an array of special groups, the two primary units assigned a counterterrorist mission are the U.S. Army's Delta Force and the U.S. Navy SEALs.

THE SECRET ARMY | Delta Force has become a critical fixture of U.S. counterterrorism. When it was formed in 1977, it was a bold new step for the national military. Delta Force arose to address increasingly brazen attacks against U.S. targets worldwide, especially in light of inadequate U.S. responses to those attacks. During the Vietnam War, several special operations attempts failed. These failures highlighted the need for more effective forces. One of the best known of these attempts was the Sontay operation to rescue U.S. prisoners of war in North Vietnam. After massive planning, the mission ended barely thirty minutes after it was launched—when Delta found no prisoners to be rescued. Somehow, critical intelligence had slipped through the cracks. This dangerous error dramatically demonstrated the need for a more systematic approach to such specialized operations. Later episodes, such as a hostage taking in Sudan and a bombing in Germany, only underscored the necessity of having forces trained specifically to handle rescues and other unconventional or counterterrorist missions.

Responding to these cues, President Jimmy Carter authorized the formation of just such a force. But the young program faced special challenges. Following the unpopular Vietnam War, many civilians and politicians had an antimilitary stance. Even top military commanders, still reeling from Vietnam, were in no mood to embark on a new plan to send U.S. forces into conflict. In addition, existing special forces feared that a new elite group would threaten their own capabilities and standing.

Nevertheless, plans for the force moved ahead. Heading the ambitious project was Colonel Charles Beckwith, who envisioned a highly capable force that would take on missions deep behind enemy lines. In 1977 the ultrasecret 1st Special Forces Operational Detachment-Delta (SFOD-D)—better known as Delta Force or simply Delta—was created.

DELTA'S DEMANDS

According to the U.S. Department of Defense and the U.S. Army, Delta does not officially exist. However, this "nonexistent" unit occasionally prints recruitment ads in various army publications. Each applicant must meet the following requirements, among others:

- Must be a male U.S. citizen with a minimum age of twenty-two
- Must be an active-duty member of the U.S. Army or a member of the U.S. Army Reserve or National Guard
- Must be airborne qualified or volunteer for airborne training
- Must pass physical and eye examinations, including clearance for HALO (high altitude low opening) parachuting and scuba (self contained underwater breathing apparatus) diving
- Must pass a background security investigation and have a security clearance of secret or higher
- Must pass the five-event physical fitness qualification test (inverted crawl; run, dodge, and jump; push-ups; sit-ups; and two-mile run) and the one-hundred-yard swim, all while wearing fatigues and boots ■

Rumored to be based at Fort Bragg, North Carolina, Delta sought members from the Army Special Forces. To mold soldiers into the elite new group, Beckwith instituted an intense nineteen-week training course.

■ ■

Delta Drills

The days dragged on, *seemingly without end. The Delta trainees had come from the most elite divisions of the U.S. military, and they were used to the difficult demands of special operations. But this was unlike anything they had ever done. Delta members had to run the farthest, shoot the best, and endure the harshest conditions. The United States would be relying upon them to be its front line in the covert counterterrorist war—an uncharted war without any rules.*

These U.S. special forces—while not officially Delta members— train at the elaborate Fort Bragg facilities used by Delta.

Predawn physical training was followed by weapons drills, forced marches, more weapons training, intelligence instruction, and then more weapons training. In addition to the merciless physical regimen, trainees were instructed in every element of counterterrorist tradecraft. They spent nearly ten hours a day perfecting assault and rescue skills. New Delta members—known as operators—learned to ski, dive, drive race cars, maneuver massive trucks, hot-wire vehicles, and pick locks. They also learned to disappear into a crowd in any foreign locale— even when they were being tailed by undercover agents.

Most of this instruction took place at Delta's elaborate training facility. The top secret complex is rumored to have an indoor firing range and a rappelling tower for practicing skills at swinging down from helicopters or rooftops on ropes. It is also said to have some of the most sophisticated sniper ranges in the world. Intensive hostage-rescue training was also conducted in fully furnished rooms populated with cardboard cutouts of hostages and terrorists, as well as flesh-and-blood Delta members. These exercises—using live fire in close quarters, where the danger of shooting a comrade was very real—disciplined both body and mind. Part of the facility was also said to house a portion of a wide-bodied airliner hung by steel cables from the ceiling. No detail was left untouched. The plane was fitted with authentic aircraft seats and mannequins dressed as holiday travelers, playing the role of hostages.

■ ■

But as rigorous as the training was, it was still just practice for the real thing. Members of the new unit craved a mission. Their first opportunity arose on November 4, 1979, when the U.S. embassy in Tehran was taken over and its staff was seized by Iran's Revolutionary Guards. Delta was placed on full alert and plans were prepared.

Assaulting the besieged embassy would be no small challenge. Operating in any enemy city required special care. But Iran, in the throes of an Islamic revolution, presented unusual obstacles. Many Iranians viewed non-Muslims and Westerners with hostility and suspicion. Blending in would not be easy.

The planned operation consisted of several elements. First, the task force needed accurate intelligence on exactly where the more than fifty U.S. hostages were being held. With that information, the force—which had to be large enough to overpower the Revolutionary Guards and free the hostages—had to be transported into Iran. Once there, the operators would still need to reach the heart of downtown Tehran. Finally, air transport would have to fly both the hostages and the rescue force to safety.

Delta clearly couldn't do the job alone. U.S. Navy vessels would be needed to transport the force to the Persian Gulf. From there, U.S. Air Force planes and U.S. Marine Corps helicopters would get the team to a staging area in the southern Iranian desert and then on into Tehran. Once

Tehran in 1979 was a hotbed of anti-U.S. sentiment. This banner denounces "Uncle Sam" and his forces, while a scrawled message on the wall below criticizes then-president Jimmy Carter.

on the ground, Beckwith would send in his unit. Meanwhile, U.S. planes would fly close cover over the city to prevent any retaliation by Iranian air force fighter jets. Finally, when the hostages were freed, choppers and planes would be used again to get all of them out of Iran.

To succeed, the complex and far-reaching mission required absolute cooperation among its players. But the various military services taking part in the operation—still less than friendly with the upstart Delta—bickered and competed. Despite the risks, Beckwith knew that the risk of inaction was far greater. But it would be nearly six months before the time for action came.

■ ■

Operation Eagle Claw

April 24, 1980, *was set as the date of the Tehran operation, code-named "Eagle Claw." A stretch of calm weather over the sands of southern Iran's desert had opened a rare—and narrow—window of opportunity for the low-flying helicopters. The Delta operators had already been ferried to the Desert One staging area by an C-130 transport plane. As they waited for the choppers that would take them to Tehran, they thought about the mission that lay ahead. They*

A hulking C-130 Hercules aircraft like this one was tasked with safely transporting Delta operators to Desert One for the Eagle Claw mission.

considered the dangers and tactical challenges of rescuing such a large group of hostages inside a turbulent city. They thought of their families. They thought of their desire to follow Chargin' Charlie's lead and to protect and save American lives.

Meanwhile, miles away over the desert, problems struck as the eight choppers struggled with a bumpy ride to the landing zone. Warm air bounced off the desert floor, whipping up the sands. The marine pilots struggled to control their aircraft amid the turbulence, knowing that the hopes of a nation were pinned on their ability to get the choppers to Iran.

But it wasn't enough. Blinding clouds of dust and sand forced two choppers to turn back. Another faced crippling mechanical problems. In the end, only five choppers arrived safely at Desert One—and Beckwith needed six to get all of his men to the rescue. It was over. Beckwith aborted the mission.

The dejected operators prepared to return to the USS Nimitz aircraft carrier waiting for them in the Persian Gulf. Suddenly, before the aircraft could taxi and take off from the makeshift desert runway, one of the helicopter pilots lost his bearings in the dark and the blowing sand. The chopper banked sharply, crashing into the parked plane. The fuel-laden aircraft exploded into flame, killing eight servicemen and wounding dozens more.

The Eagle Claw mission had ended in disaster before it had even really begun. The hostages had been scattered to various locations throughout Iran, and the young Delta Force had been dealt a damaging blow.

■ ■

If nothing else, the Eagle Claw disaster proved that the United States could no longer allow interservice competition and bureaucracy to hinder its counterterrorism efforts. Significant changes soon took place in the special operations community. By 1981 the government had formed the Joint Special Operations Command to manage U.S. counterterrorist forces. Meanwhile, Delta expanded in both size and capabilities.

But Delta's operational experience remained limited. Although the unit was called to assault a hijacked Kuwaiti Airlines jet in 1984, complications at Fort Bragg ultimately prevented Delta's deployment. The next opportunity for action came on June 14, 1985, when Hezbollah terrorists hijacked TWA Flight 847 from Athens, Greece, and commandeered it to Algiers, Algeria. Delta operators were immediately placed on maximum alert and deployed to Algiers. However, once there, Algerian authorities refused to let Delta operate on the nation's soil. As Delta sat powerless—and as U.S. president Ronald Reagan declared that

Two masked Hezbollah terrorists stand outside the hijacked TWA plane, which is parked on a Beirut tarmac before heading to Algiers. Delta operators were eager to recapture the jet, but their efforts were thwarted.

the United States would not negotiate with terrorists—the Hezbollah operatives brutally murdered a young U.S. Navy diver named Robert Dean Stethem.

Delta's next major operation in the Middle East was no more successful. On October 7, 1985, four terrorists from the Palestine Liberation Front (PLF) seized the Italian cruise ship *Achille Lauro* during a Mediterranean voyage. Over the next two days, the Palestinians tormented the crew and about four hundred passengers, many of whom were Jewish. One of these passengers was Leon Klinghoffer, a sixty-nine-year-old wheelchair-bound American Jew. Off the coast of Syria, the terrorists shot Klinghoffer in the head at point-blank range and tossed his body and wheelchair into the Mediterranean.

Delta was again called upon to counter the terrorist threat. But, once again, the unit's efforts were compromised by international power struggles. To end the ordeal, Egyptian president Hosni Mubarak arranged for the terrorists to surrender to Egypt in exchange for being flown out of Egypt, along with the group's leader, Abu Abbas. But U.S. authorities had no intention of letting the hijackers go free—especially after a report from Nicholas Veliotes, the U.S. ambassador to Egypt. Veliotes had boarded the ship to see how the American citizens on board had been treated. When he discovered that Leon Klinghoffer had been murdered by the terrorists, he radioed his aide onshore with the terrible news.

Acting on this information, U.S. Navy F-14s intercepted the EgyptAir jet carrying the Palestinians and forced it to land at Sigonella Naval Air Station in Sicily, Italy. A team of Delta operators waited in Sicily to take down the aircraft. Their goal was to bring the terrorists into custody.

A formation of F-14s rises against a clear sky. These swift fighter planes were deployed to intercept the hijackers' flight from Egypt.

Showdown in Sicily

The Boeing jet, decorated with EgyptAir's trademark red, black, and yellow, rolled to a slow halt on the Sigonella tarmac. Three sniper teams, their long guns focused on the cockpit, radioed in the exact position of the aircraft as the section commander reviewed intelligence reports. About a dozen men were believed to be aboard the aircraft: the four hijackers, Abu Abbas, the plane's crew, and a few Egyptian security agents. But important questions remained. How many of them were armed? Would they resist or surrender?

The operators surrounding the plane weren't taking any chances. The motto of "never bring a knife to a gunfight" had kept Delta members alive time and again. As the aircraft's engines whirred to a stop, the operators leaped into place on the jet, assuming firing positions on the wings and around the main cabin doors. Their MP5 submachine guns were locked and loaded, ready to fire if the door swung open and the terrorists offered a challenge. The operators were

Italian police cluster around Youssef Magied al-Molqi, one of the *Achille Lauro* hijackers. Delta was once again prevented from completing its intended rescue mission.

also braced to storm the aircraft if necessary. The terrorists would not be allowed to take a second group of captives—not on Delta's watch.

Suddenly, sirens sounded in the distance and a convoy of carabinieri (national Italian police) swung into view. The Delta *members felt their spirits sink. Following urgent instructions from Rome, the carabinieri prevented Delta from acting. After a bitter tug of war that almost developed into a full-fledged fight, the Italians arrested the* Achille Lauro *hijackers and allowed Abu Abbas to go free. The chance to bring four killers to justice faded in the glare of the Italian police lights, and Delta went home empty-handed.*

■ ■

Despite yet another thwarted mission, Delta remained active. In the Middle East, Delta operators executed covert actions in search of U.S. hostages in Lebanon. In Latin America, Delta engaged in a host of counternarcotics raids and other operations. One of the unit's most dramatic missions in the region took place in Panama in 1989. Under the rule of the dictator Manuel Noriega, an American named Kurt Muse had been arrested for running an underground radio station that criticized the government. After harsh interrogation, Muse was confined for nine months to a cell in the brutal, overcrowded Carcel Modelo (Model Prison). Determined to get him out, a force of Delta operators and members of other military branches carried out a mission called Operation Just Cause. The U.S. operators stormed the prison and rescued Muse, marking the first time in history that a U.S. hostage had been rescued.

However, Delta's most highly publicized international deployment was to the East

Noriega *(above)* arrested hundreds of political prisoners during his reign.

African nation of Somalia in 1993. The 75th Ranger Regiment (Airborne) and other elements of the U.S. military were already in Somalia, hoping to apprehend Mohamed Farrah Aidid, a warlord who had used starvation as a tool of terror against his own people. Delta's counterterrorist skills and its ability to blend into a hostile environment were ideal for the close-quarter urban combat that was typical in the Somalian capital of Mogadishu. That summer, Delta joined its comrades in East Africa.

On October 3, 1993, six Black Hawk choppers and four MH-6 Little Birds flew a force of approximately one hundred U.S. Army Rangers and Delta operators into downtown Mogadishu. A fleet of massive humvee vehicles, two more Black Hawks, and four rocket-bearing AH-6 Little Birds backed up the force as it descended on the Olympic Hotel in an attempt to seize Aidid. Commandos stormed the hotel, some racing in on the ground and others swinging down from the choppers on dangling ropes. The team swiftly captured about twenty of Aidid's top lieutenants. But when Somali gunners fired rocket-propelled grenades at the hovering Hawks, two were shot down and a third was damaged.

U.S. soldiers and UN peacekeepers in Mogadishu were joined by Delta operators intent on capturing Aidid, but the mission ended in tragedy.

An eighteen-hour battle ensued in the streets—one of the largest fought by U.S. forces since Vietnam. Early in the morning of October 4, a rescue convoy made it to the scene and carried most of the force to safety. But eighteen U.S. servicepeople—and several hundred Somalis—were dead.

INTO AFGHANISTAN
Following the tragedy in Somalia, Delta's profile once again sank below the public view for some time. But in the wake of September 11, 2001, Delta reappeared on the

counterterrorism scene. When the U.S. military sent forces to Afghanistan to hunt down the the al-Qaeda leaders who were based there, Delta teams were among the first to go.

■ ■

Night Mission

The darkness was heavy, *the terrain treacherous. But the operators' years of training at Fort Bragg had prepared them for this type of brutal, merciless warfare and for the harsh conditions in which the battle was to be waged. Making their way down a mountain path that was dangerous even in the daytime, the team moved slowly and soundlessly. Even the M4 carbines and M21 sniper rifles slung over their shoulders were suppressed with silencers. The operators followed night-vision strobes on the backs of each other's helmets—essential equipment in avoiding stumbling and compromising the team.*

The operators' mission in the mountains north of Peshawar, Pakistan, was a direct action response to the challenge al-Qaeda presented to U.S. national security. It was also payback. Marching briskly in a tight, disciplined formation, the operators stalked their prey with two objectives in mind. If they surrender, capture them; if they resist, execute them. As the team neared its target—a cave chiseled into the side of a mountain—an Arabic-speaking operator used a bullhorn to demand that anyone inside surrender or face death. When the ultimatum went unheeded, the team moved in for the kill.

■ ■

Even as Delta moves out of the shadows and onto the front lines, many of their exact missions—such as the one above—are still top secret. But within days of the devastating attacks against New York City and Washington, D.C., Delta advance teams were on the ground in Afghanistan. As the best-trained unit in the U.S. military, Delta was ideally suited for the worldwide conflict that had become known as the War on Terror. Beyond their hostage-rescue and assault skills, Delta operators had trained in extreme weather and terrain. They could be helicoptered into an area in the middle of the night to face an unseen foe or to parachute deep into terrorist-controlled territory. But the unit's true strength—and what made it such an effective tool against an enemy as entrenched as al-Qaeda—was its ability to search for, locate, monitor, track, and capture wanted individuals.

That ability was put to good use in Afghanistan. Working with the CIA and the military, Delta launched a massive manhunt operation to rid Afghanistan and the Pakistani border of al-Qaeda operativs.

But these critical operations came at a price. On October 12, 2001, Delta operators engaged in a fierce, close-quarter fight with members of al-Qaeda and of the Taliban (a radical Islamic government that supported al-Qaeda) near Kandahar, Afghanistan. The enemy put up a fierce resistance, wounding twelve Delta members in the battle.

| THE NAVY'S BEST | As varied as Delta's capabilities and global reach are, the unit is only responsible for counterterrorist operations *above* the waterline. Maritime counterterrorism in the U.S. military is the domain of the U.S. Navy's Sea, Air, Land Teams, usually known simply as Navy SEALs.

The first SEAL teams had been formed in 1962 as part of President Kennedy's drive to increase the military's special operations.

Navy SEALs endure months of grueling training to join one of the nation's most elite special forces.

THE ONLY EASY DAY
WAS YESTERDAY

Becoming a member of a U.S. Navy SEAL team is one of the most difficult achievements in the U.S. military. In fact, SEALs' selection and training is considered among the toughest in the world. After a seven-week period to weed out less-dedicated candidates, potential SEALs undergo the notorious Basic Underwater Demolitions/SEAL (BUD/S) training, which can last from seven months to two years. The program has a 60 percent dropout rate.

The first phase of BUD/S is physical conditioning. It is also in this phase that candidates learn the essentials of teamwork. Phase One of BUD/S culminates in the infamous six-day "Hell Week," during which the candidates are pushed to the edge of physical and mental endurance. Much of the strenuous physical examination is done with no sleep. Phase Two is the underwater and scuba course. Much of this phases's emphasis is on diving, equipment, and other aspects of underwater warfare.

The third and final phase is the land warfare section, which involves both underwater infiltration and land warfare skills. The exact curriculum of this third phase is classified information. However, the training is believed to include basic weaponry, marksmanship, combat shooting, explosive charges handling, and sabotage techniques, as well as night fighting, ambushing, and patrolling. Long-range reconnaissance, intelligence gathering, and communications and radio procedures are also part of the basics. Helicopter insertion and extraction and small-unit tactics and skills round out the curriculum. In this final phase, trainees are introduced to the force's advanced fleet of special operations submarines, high-speed boats, and other watercraft. Candidates also officially become active members, or operatives, in this final phase.

Upon successful completion of BUD/S, the new operatives are sent to U.S. Army Jump School at Fort Benning, Georgia, and then on to six-week probationary periods with their teams. Next, in SEAL Tactical Training—an advanced version of Phase Three—SEALs study and master the intricacies of the team's operational procedures. Finally, each member is awarded the Trident (the SEALs' emblem) in an emotional and highly secret ceremony. The Trident is the ultimate symbol of a SEAL's worth and may be the most coveted insignia in the entire U.S. Navy. The SEALs began as the best of the best in the U.S. military, and that tradition continues. ∎

As with many of the early groups that were formed to handle unconventional warfare, the SEALs' initial focus was not counterterrorism. Their baptism of fire had been in the seas, rivers, and rice paddies of Vietnam. Their ability to pop up along a darkened North Vietnamese shoreline, evade sentries, and capture or eliminate targets deep behind enemy lines soon became legendary. Most of their enemies never knew what hit them. Organized into distinct teams—each responsible for operations in a different part of the world—they numbered only a few hundred men. Nevertheless, the SEALs proved to be an enormous asset to the U.S. military.

As counterterrorism became an even more pressing issue, SEALs teams were increasingly called upon to respond to threats alongside Delta and other special forces. The SEALs' many strengths—the unit's cohesion, a highly accurate intelligence network, stealthy assaults, and stunning versatility—would serve them well in counterterrorist operations. In fact, SEAL team members took part in one of Delta's early raids—the failed mission to rescue U.S. hostages from Tehran.

Immediately following that failed attempt, the U.S. Navy created a new SEAL team, called SEAL Team SIX. Like Delta, this men-only team would be placed on permanent alert and was dedicated specifically to responding to terrorist attacks against U.S. targets. The man tasked with creating Team SIX was Richard Marcinko.

Under Marcinko, training for the navy's counterterrorist unit was grueling. Operatives were expected to perform exceptionally in any environment, from South American rivers to the shoreline of the Persian Gulf. A particular emphasis of SEAL Team SIX training was hostage rescue. Members were drilled in the basics of storming a seized offshore oil platform, reaching a hijacked passenger liner, or taking back a captured naval vessel.

The rigorous training would not go to waste. Throughout the 1980s and 1990s, SEAL Team SIX was summoned to cases of maritime terrorism including the 1985 seizure of the *Achille Lauro*. That same year, Team SIX was also called to the rescue of the hijacked TWA Flight 847. Because the plane was briefly held at Beirut International Airport, which straddled the Mediterranean, a rescue force was deployed along the shoreline. The attempt ultimately failed. But the SEALs were not discouraged and soon attempted another Middle East rescue.

■ ■

Underwater Warriors

The Mediterranean was calm that dark night—but, then, the seas were always placid thirty feet below the waves. Swimmer Delivery Vehicles (SDVs), which resembled oversized torpedoes, carried several SEALs to the Lebanese shoreline. They wore full scuba gear, while rebreathers ensured that the bubbles from their breathing gear didn't reach the surface.

The operatives were headed into the lion's den of Beirut—a headquarters of international terrorism in the 1980s. Hezbollah had abducted several U.S. citizens, including CIA station chief William Buckley. But the group's 1983 bombing of the U.S. embassy, which had killed many of the post's intelligence chiefs, had severely damaged the United States' ability to monitor the group. As a result, intelligence on where the hostages might be was sorely lacking. After landing, the SEALs team was to search the city's slums for Hezbollah strongholds where the American hostages might be held.

Once the SDVs dropped them on a secluded beach, the commandos would change into camouflaged fatigues and remove their AK-47s and M16s from their waterproof wrapping. Silenced 9mm pistols were concealed inside holsters, and razor-sharp daggers had been stowed in boots. The mission was rife with danger—especially since U.S. special forces were not supposed to be operating inside Lebanon—but members of the U.S. Navy's counterterrorist unit were trained to be ready for anything. Nevertheless, all of their skills and dedication could not bring them success on this chilly fall night.

A Navy SEAL in full scuba gear emerges from the waves armed and ready for action.

Struggling against overwhelming dangers and obstacles to their search, the SEALs were forced to withdraw without the hostages.

■ ■

Like Delta Force, SEAL Team SIX—while it remains deeply covert—is no longer unknown to civilians. Delta operators have traveled throughout the Middle East, the Caribbean, and Latin America. In recent years, the unit has served in the Persian Gulf during the 1990 and 2003 wars with Iraq, and it often works as a protection force to monitor possible terrorist activity. However, much of the work surrounding SEAL missions is still shrouded in absolute secrecy.

| **JOINING FORCES** | As the U.S. response to terrorism grew both more specialized and more coordinated following September 11, units such as Delta and the SEALs began working together more closely and more often. A prime example of such collaboration was born out of a U.S.-led war launched against Iraq in March 2003. The war was based on suspicions that Iraqi president and dictator Saddam Hussein had weapons of mass destruction, which he might make available to terrorists. Several international terrorists were also found in the country.

However, the arrival of U.S. troops—and their ongoing presence after the official end of major combat in May 2003—aroused strong anti-American feeling throughout the Middle East. Iraq's volatile postwar state soon proved to be a perfect breeding ground for new and increased terrorist activity. Car bombings, drive-by shootings, and similar attacks targeted U.S. troops and other Westerners in Iraq, especially in the capital city of Baghdad. These attacks were thought to be carried out by former members of Hussein's administration, army, and political party. While Hussein himself had gone into hiding in April after the fall of Baghdad, he may have been directing or encouraging the guerilla-style onslaught. Terrorists from other Middle Eastern nations were also suspected of entering Iraq to carry out strikes.

To counter these and other threats, the U.S. government created Task Force 121 in November 2003. This group brought together elements of Delta Force, the SEALs, the CIA, and other U.S. military and intelligence groups. Able to act quickly and precisely by coordinating efforts and information, the covert unit was given the mission of hunting down high-profile targets in Iraq and the surrounding region. In addition to Hussein and his top aides, these targets included Osama bin Laden and al-Qaeda operatives.

Joining the already enormous manhunt for Hussein—who had been dubbed High Value Target Number One—Task Force 121 soon got the chance to prove itself. On December 13, the unit took part in a critical raid code-named Operation Red Dawn. Along with some six hundred other troops, the force finally tracked down Hussein in central Iraq. They found him hiding in a "spider hole," a narrow underground

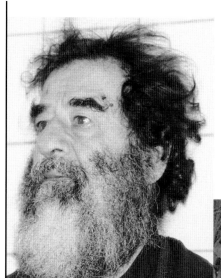

shaft only large enough for one person. The former president was taken into custody, and Task Force 121 celebrated a major success. With such a victory already achieved, joining forces in this way is likely to grow more and more common in the future.

Members of Task Force 121 helped capture a disheveled Saddam Hussein *(upper left)* in a cramped and dirty hideout, which was no more than a narrow shaft hidden by a makeshift Styrofoam lid *(above)*.

In the Shadows:
The Central Intelligence Agency

Backing up the military in the War on Terror is a wide intelligence network. Heading this community is the CIA, the foreign intelligence-gathering and analysis arm of the U.S. government. Its job is to collect, evaluate, and disseminate foreign intelligence on targets and countries around the world. The president and other high-level officials then use this intelligence in making national security decisions.

The CIA employs a far-reaching series of measures to gather this critical information. The process begins near the surface, with reviews and analysis of open-source material such as newspapers, broadcasts, and speeches. Often, however, open sources only provide the basics—a road

CIA headquarters in Langley, Virginia

map of sorts—but not enough data for the president and other members of the national security staff to use in policy making. The CIA also relies on electronic and high-tech tools, such as phone taps and radio intercepts. A newer counterterrorism tactic focuses on preventing cyberterrorism—attacks launched over the Internet or through other computer-related channels. Further data comes from other U.S. intelligence-gathering agencies and from the U.S. military. And, finally, the CIA employs agents to gather intelligence and to protect the interests of the United States. These agents—also called operatives or spies—are stationed throughout the world.

Beginning in the late 1990s, the CIA's Special Operations Group (SOG) began taking a greater role in the agency's activity. And in the wake of September 11, the CIA and its covert special operations force has become one of the United States' most active and most secretive counterterrorist forces. As the global threat from al-Qaeda and the Islamic fundamentalist terrorism network took center stage, the SOG really went to war, and it has remained in the vanguard of the U.S. War on Terror.

| BUILDING THE SOG |

Although the SOG has gained new prominence, the concept behind it dates back to World War II. At that time, the director of the Office of Strategic Services (the forerunner of the CIA) and OSS founder William "Wild Bill" Donovan created a force of deep-cover agents to carry out intelligence-gathering and espionage assignments. The philosophy behind the SOG during wartime was to create confusion, destruction, and fear among the enemy.

Having seen the value of such a force as the SOG, President Harry Truman signed the National Security Act on July 26, 1947, creating the CIA. Since then, the CIA has executed covert intelligence-gathering and paramilitary operations against U.S. enemies or in support of U.S. allies.

OSS creator and head Major General William "Wild Bill" Donovan

In one such mission, in August 1953, the CIA helped to engineer a coup against Iran's premier Mohammad Mosaddeq that restored the pro-American shah to the throne. Most famously, however, in April 1961, a force of CIA-trained Cuban exiles landed at the Bay of Pigs and invaded Communist Cuba—only to be soundly defeated. The incident was a humiliating loss for the CIA. But it did not end the CIA's global covert war, and operations continued around the world, from Latin America to Southeast Asia. But it gradually became clear that too many of these operations were failing, playing out unpredictably, or setting off dangerous chain reactions within unstable nations. In 1975 Senate hearings investigated CIA practices and ultimately ended most of the agency's covert operations and unconventional methods. For the time being, the CIA had lost its capability to wage secretive wars on a global scale.

| OLD ENEMIES, NEW ALLIES | A new wrinkle in global

politics appeared in 1979, when Soviet troops invaded Afghanistan and war erupted. With the Cold War still at a fever pitch, the United States was eager to combat Soviet aggression and to thwart Soviet power wherever it surfaced. CIA agents soon traveled to Afghanistan to form alliances with the mujahideen (Islamic warriors) battling the Soviets.

■ ■

With the Mujahideen

The CIA agents *hardly seemed like potential allies to the mujahideen. That ragtag band of warriors was engaged in a jihad (holy struggle) against the Soviets in part because the invaders were non-Muslim outsiders, much like the U.S. agents themselves. For their part, the men from the CIA were trained in all areas of intelligence tradecraft, but nothing could have fully prepared them for this mission. The unfamiliar landscape of Afghanistan and Pakistan— filled with windswept plains, rocky peaks, and ancient ruins—was harsh, alien, and frequently beautiful. Their new brothers in arms, too, seemed deeply foreign to the CIA operatives. With their striking features, traditional flowing dress, and a fierce dedication, the mujahideen seemed closer to ancient tribal warriors than to the clean-cut CIA agents. Nevertheless, employing the ancient philosophy that "the enemy of my enemy is my friend," the CIA and the mujahideen forged an uneasy partnership to force the Soviets out of Afghanistan.*

The CIA provided arms, funds, and training to the native Afghans, making sure that they had whatever they needed to fight.

Mujahideen build bombs by lamplight. During the Soviet war, CIA agents provided Afghan forces with extensive training and funding.

In addition, the CIA also built strong links with Arab volunteers who flocked to Afghanistan from around the region to join in the jihad. The U.S. agents saw, firsthand, the ferocious intensity that these holy warriors displayed on the battlefield. In fact, the CIA trained many of them in the use of explosives and antitank and antiaircraft missiles, as well as the darker arts of subversive warfare and special operations. These skills included reconnaissance, ambushing, assassination, and kidnapping.

The war in Afghanistan would drag on for a long and brutal decade. For the CIA agents on the ground, victory was measured bullet by bullet and day by day. But the Afghan forces finally won— thanks in no small part to the CIA's help.

Ironically, the Afghan war would eventually help to create the international network of fundamentalist Islamic terrorism. Some of the mujahideen decided to carry the jihad beyond Afghanistan and to attack non-Muslim nations and interests wherever they were seen to threaten the Islamic world. One of the most determined and ambitious of these men was Osama bin Laden, who went on to found al-Qaeda.

NEW AND IMPROVED | Just as CIA efforts in Afghanistan indirectly trained and funded future al-Qaeda members, the rising threat of Islamic terrorism from al-Qaeda and other groups eventually sparked the resurgence of the CIA's covert operations. The rebirth of the CIA's special operations apparatus came about in 1997, when George Tenet became the CIA's director. At the time, the CIA was monitoring attempts by Hezbollah, al-Qaeda, and other Middle Eastern groups to extend the terrorist network into Europe using the unstable and war-torn nations of the region as a channel. However, the CIA's SOG force was not large enough to operate effectively. Seeing a need for improved U.S. intelligence and special operations capability, Tenet saw to it that the CIA's modern SOG became one of the best-equipped and most generously funded counterterrorist forces in the world.

CIA director George Tenet expanded the SOG but later came under attack for mishandling intelligence.

Tenet began recruiting SOG agents from the ranks of the U.S. Army and Navy counterterrorist teams, as well as other branches of the U.S. military special operations community and from within the CIA. The exact qualifications to be in SOG are classified, but it is known that only operatives of exceptional physical and psychological strength are selected—the very best of the best. New recruits in the CIA's covert army are trained at a state-of-the-art tradecraft school at Camp Peary, Virginia. SOG operatives must know how to do anything in the field, from kidnapping the wife of a terrorist chieftain to storming a plane full of hostages. The specific courses at Camp Peary are top secret, but the training is a hands-on and often harsh introduction to the realities of operating in a hostile environment. According to reports, a team can be as large as twenty people or as small as just one agent sent deep behind enemy lines. Members learn that all they can count on is their wits, their .45 caliber handgun, and their survival skills to evade capture. And if they are captured, they must have the strength to withstand torture.

The SOG consists of ground, maritime, and air branches. The Ground Branch, the group's largest, consists of the commandos—agents who infiltrate enemy territory to carry out direct action assignments. Although each and every member of the Ground Branch is a spy well versed in the art of intelligence tradecraft, the emphasis in this section is on firearms and commando techniques. Small arms proficiency—from a 9mm pistol to a 7.62mm machine gun—is a must for all SOG agents, as well as skills in close-quarter battle, sniping and countersniping, improvised explosives, and bomb disposal.

Specialized driving is another essential skill taught to Ground Branch members. Whether at the wheel of a luxury car on the midday streets of Paris or using night-vision goggles to steer a rickety jeep through

APPLICANTS WANTED

Looking for a job with a good salary, lots of travel, and the chance to meet interesting people? The CIA has an offer for you. According to official recruiting material, men and women seeking careers in intelligence work should be self-reliant, responsible, adventurous, tough, intellectual, and trustworthy. Specific qualifications to be accepted into the CIA's Clandestine Service Trainee Program include:

- U.S. citizenship
- Age under thirty-five
- A bachelor's degree and an excellent academic record
- Strong interpersonal skills and the ability to communicate clearly and accurately
- A burning interest in international affairs

The CIA is particularly interested in candidates with backgrounds in Central Eurasian, East Asian, and Middle Eastern languages—areas in which the program is still weak. Experience living abroad, military service, and graduate degrees—especially in international economics, international business, or the physical sciences—are desirable. In addition, all applicants must pass medical and psychological exams, polygraph (lie detector) interviews, and background checks. ∎

the muddy hills near Peshawar, commandos must be able to pursue enemies or flee from threats. Ground Branch members are also trained to blend seamlessly into large crowds, to gather intelligence from a scene, and to use unarmed combat techniques to capture or subdue individuals.

| **ON THE FRONT LINES** | When al-Qaeda brought its global jihad to the United States on September 11, 2001, the CIA went into immediate action. SOG Ground Branch agents were dispatched from CIA headquarters in Langley and rushed to Afghanistan as the rubble still smoldered at ground zero. They hoped to reestablish links with some of the CIA's Afghan allies of twenty years earlier, many of whom opposed bin Laden and his Taliban protectors. But these agents were a different breed than those who had first worked alongside the mujahideen. These SOG members were tactically trained commandos, experienced in the brutal art of counterterrorism.

■ ■

Back to Afghanistan
SOG "uniforms" were never really uniform. *Most agents wore jeans, T-shirts, local headgear, and the best holsters the CIA budget would allow. Shaving was rarely a priority. Neither was bathing. And meals were hardly luxurious. In the Afghan mountains,*

After 9/11 the SOG joined forces with Northern Alliance members (*above*), many of whom were former mujahideen, to fight the Taliban.

where the only supplies were dropped by air, the team survived on PowerBars and purified water carried on the backs of donkeys.

But these ragged-looking agents were waging a critical war, one far off the beaten path of the U.S. military effort. Operating independently and well below the radar of the more conventional forces in Afghanistan, the SOG's mission was to locate, seize, and interrogate al-Qaeda commanders and other terrorist operatives who could provide invaluable intelligence.

The SOG teams had come to Afghanistan with a knowledge of local languages and dialects, plus plenty of CIA cash and weapons to engage al-Qaeda and Taliban forces in unconventional battle. The agents were masterful fighters, and their weapons proficiency was matched by their close-combat skills and ruthless determination. They were feared by al-Qaeda members, who moved from place to place during the night to avoid capture or death. Nearly as important as the CIA agents' mission to capture was their mission to instill fear in the hearts of the terrorists, to make it absolutely clear that the United States would not be defeated by terror.

The SOG's operations in Afghanistan were sometimes deadly. On November 29, 2001, Johnny "Mike" Spann, a thirty-year-old SOG agent, was killed at the Kala Jangi fortress, where he had been interrogating captured al-Qaeda and Taliban operatives. The prisoners had revolted and a vicious fight had ensued. But the SOG would remain in Afghanistan to carry out its mission.

SOG agent
Johnny "Mike" Spann

| FROM SEA TO SKY | The

SOG also has a Maritime Branch, made up primarily of former Navy SEALs and U.S. Marines. These agents are trained in the use of unconventional means and tools—from jet skis to smuggling boats—to infiltrate enemy waters. The Maritime Branch also uses seafaring cargo ships and passenger liners to fulfill its objectives and missions.

Last but not least is the Air Branch, which has been the SOG's most prominent unit since September 11. Pilots are trained to fly virtually anything—from antique Soviet helicopters to passenger jets. The Air Branch owes its legacy to Air America, a paramilitary air force used in Vietnam to bomb targets, supply weapons, and otherwise aid in the CIA's covert operations in Southeast Asia. Forty years later, the Air Branch took a similar role in Afghanistan and throughout the Middle East. Capable of transporting operatives and tracking al-Qaeda commanders on the run, the Air Branch also had a unique new tool to hunt down terrorists with pinpoint precision: unmanned aerial vehicles (UAVs), also called drones.

One of these UAVs was buzzing softly through the night sky

A SOG Predator drone killed top al-Qaeda lieutenant Mohammed Atef, a close aide to bin Laden.

approximately five thousand feet above southeastern Afghanistan's mountains in November 2001. Osama bin Laden and several of his top lieutenants were taking shelter there from U.S. bombing strikes. With deadly accuracy, the unmanned Predator drone launched an AGM-114 Hellfire missile into the camp where Mohammed Atef, al-Qaeda's military commander, was hidden. The missile—designed to slice through enemy armor—killed Atef and several members of his group.

One year later, on November 3, 2002, another SOG Air Branch Predator drone launched a Hellfire missile at a vehicle traveling in the deserts of Yemen. The vehicle carried Ali Qaed Sunian al-Harithi, better known as Abu Ali. A top lieutenant of bin Laden's, Ali was one of the masterminds behind the October 2000 bombing of the USS *Cole* in the Yemeni port of Aden. He was killed in the strike, along with five passengers riding with him, all of them al-Qaeda operatives.

In March 2003, SOG members were on yet another hunt. The agency had been looking for Khalid Shaikh Mohammed for nearly a decade—ever since he had plotted to destroy eleven U.S. airliners over the Pacific and to crash a hijacked Boeing 747 into CIA headquarters. Thought to be the third-highest man in al-Qaeda's hierarchy, the target had also been a key player in bombings of two U.S. embassies in Kenya and Tanzania in 1998, as well as the *Cole* bombing. But his biggest crime was his role in planning the September 11 attacks. In total, Mohammed had played a part in the deaths of more than three thousand people and the planned murder of many thousands more.

A price of $25 million was on the target's head, dead or alive. But alive was better. Alive, he could share a wealth of intelligence data about al-Qaeda's infrastructure, its international network, and its future operations. The CIA was determined to bring in this high-profile target.

■ ■

On the Trail of a Killer
The men moving through the quiet streets of Rawalpindi, Pakistan, sported an odd mixture of uniforms and gear. Some wore traditional military gear, with khaki drill pants, polo shirts, buzz-cut hair, and MP5 submachine guns. Others had long hair and wild, unkempt beards and carried M4 assault rifles with night-vision scopes slung over their jean jackets. Some had been hunting bin Laden and his underground army for many months. They donned the local salwar kameez—long, roomy tunics over loose pants. All of them were poised for action.

They knew that surprise was absolutely essential if the mission were going to succeed. The assault plan was simple. After hours of covertly staking out the location to make certain that the target was inside, the assault force would storm the building. They would not leave until their prey was cuffed or killed.

A few hours before dawn on March 2, 2003, as neighborhood dogs roamed the alleyways looking for scraps of food, the assembled force set off explosives that blew the fortified door off its hinges. They entered the house in a rush of swift but well-coordinated movement. Rooms were rapidly searched and deemed secure by an agent yelling "clear!" Within moments the agents found the target in the bedroom, asleep on

Khalid Shaikh Mohammed was a valuable catch for the SOG.

a mattress on the floor. They swept in, handcuffed him, and photographed him with a digital camera before pulling a black hood over his head. The team leader, using a secure satellite phone, called CIA headquarters in Langley, Virginia, to tell his bosses that Khalid Shaikh Mohammed, mastermind of September 11, was in U.S. custody.

As the target lay on the ground, bound and gagged, the agents piled into the room to catch a glimpse. They wanted to see with their own eyes one of the men who had declared war against their country.

■ ■

The SOG's capture of Khalid Shaikh Mohammed marked one of the most important victories in the War on Terror, putting the CIA's counterterrorism role into a global spotlight. But the war is far from over, and the agency's job remains a tough—and critical—element of the battle.

NATIONAL SECURITY:
OTHER FEDERAL
COUNTERTERRORIST GROUPS

U.S. military, paramilitary, and intelligence forces mostly focus on threats from outside the country. However, a host of agencies and organizations also confront terrorist threats from inside the United States. The duties of these groups range from federal law enforcement to domestic hostage rescue to developing overarching new strategies in the fight on terror. Some of these activities do eventually take them beyond U.S. borders.

| **DIPLOMATIC SECURITY SERVICE** | One important federal group is the Diplomatic Security Service (DSS), which acts as the law enforcement branch of the U.S. Department of State. The State Department originally set up its internal security arm—the forerunner of the DSS—in 1916. Its task was to carry out undercover investigations of foreign agents within the United States. The unit eventually took on responsibilities for protecting official visitors to the United States, investigating passport fraud, and maintaining security of certain government facilities.

In the 1970s and 1980s, an eruption of terrorist activity forced the State Department to reexamine its internal security. Between 1979 and 1984, hundreds of terrorist attacks were directed against U.S. citizens. Embassies were assaulted and bombed, and scores of U.S. citizens were kidnapped and killed. Partly in response to such attacks, the State Department increased security staff, updated equipment, and expanded training to include counterterrorism curricula. On November 4, 1985, the modern Diplomatic Security Service was officially created.

MORE FROM THE FEDS

Other federal groups battling terrorism against the United States include:

- **Marshals Service Special Operations Group:** The U.S. Marshals SOG is a specially trained tactical unit capable of responding to emergencies anywhere in the United States within six hours of an order. The unit is tasked with apprehending the most dangerous fugitives, including terrorists, as well as providing security to courthouses where terrorist trials are being held.
- **Secret Service:** Secret Service agents are tasked with protecting the president, vice president, their family members, and other high-profile figures who might be at risk of assassination. Various units within the Secret Service provide extra counterterrorist and counterassassination capability, including the finest snipers and countersnipers in U.S. law enforcement.
- **U.S. Coast Guard Marine Safety and Security Teams (MSSTs):** The Coast Guard's MSSTs were created after September 11 to apprehend terrorists attempting to enter the United States by sea. Ferried by high-speed boats that military planes can transport to any port, these teams intercept suspicious ships before they reach U.S. waters. ∎

Fielding a force of 1,200 federal agents, the DSS posts members to 22 domestic field offices and to more than 150 embassies and consulates around the world. Domestically, the DSS still investigates cases of passport fraud and provides protection to officials, royalty, and other high-risk targets visiting the United States. Overseas, DSS special agents serve as regional security officers (RSOs) and assistant RSOs at U.S. diplomatic posts around the globe.

RSOs are responsible for security at U.S. embassies, acting both as guards and as U.S. law enforcement contacts with local law enforcement. Often posted in countries where terrorists operate, DSS agents are on the front lines of the U.S. war against terrorism.

In February 1995, two assistant RSOs at the U.S. embassy in Islamabad, Pakistan, learned through an informant that Ramzi Yousef was in the city. As the mastermind behind the first bombing of the World Trade Center, on February 26, 1993, Yousef was a highly sought-after criminal. With the support of the FBI and Pakistani security services, the DSS tracked him down.

■ ■

Capture in Islamabad

Calls to prayer drifted through the February morning sky in 1995. For the two DSS agents, the past ninety-six hours had been a roller-coaster ride of anticipation, fear, and exhaustion. When the men had been assigned to the sprawling U.S. embassy in Pakistan, they had known that they were traveling to a turbulent nation. Yet they never expected to play a major part in the arrest of Ramzi Yousef.

Few targets were as wanted as this notorious lieutenant of Osama bin Laden. Under interrogation, Yousef had proudly admitted that he had hoped to kill 250,000 Americans in the 1993 bombing of the World Trade Center. Under his direction, al-Qaeda operatives parked a truck full of explosives in a garage under the twin towers. When the bombs went off, 6 people were killed, more than 1,000 were injured, and the building was badly damaged. Yousef shot to the top of the FBI's "Most Wanted" List and acquired a price of $2 million on his head.

Months before the DSS captured Yousef, the CIA had distributed hundreds of matchbooks bearing his face and a wanted announcement in an innovative campaign to apprehend him.

On February 7, 1995, a long trail of evidence finally led DSS and FBI agents to a guesthouse—paid for by bin Laden—in Islamabad. Yousef was swiftly arrested. But no one relaxed just yet. As they waited for the arrival of the U.S. Air Force transport that would carry Yousef to the United States for trial, the DSS agents remained alert. They knew all too well that, in a nation as volatile as Pakistan, letting down their guard was simply not an option. Yousef *could not be considered safely in the hands of U.S. justice until the plane landed in New York. Nevertheless, the agents couldn't help but feel proud—and a little relieved—after successfully handing Yousef over to the FBI. Another enemy of the United States had been caught.*

■ ■

The DSS also heads an Office of Mobile Security to counter threats at home and abroad. Special agents within this division make up Mobile Tactical Support teams, an elite force on call to respond to terrorist attacks against Americans anywhere in the world. Some of its four- to eight-member teams are quick-response units that can be deployed to posts within twenty-four hours. Agents are trained and certified as instructors in a variety of areas, and frequent missions include providing protective security for ambassadors or other senior diplomatic personnel, providing surveillance detection support, and assisting with evacuations of threatened posts.

Many of the teams' emergency response assignments have been in Africa and the Middle East, including an August 1998 mission following bombings of the U.S. embassies in Nairobi, Kenya, and Dar es Salaam, Tanzania. DSS teams also traveled to Yemen in October 2000, following the bombing of the USS *Cole.* Agents then stayed on in Yemen to protect

A gaping hole in the side of the USS *Cole* is stark evidence of another terrorist attack on U.S. forces.

FBI investigators and to bulk up security at the U.S. embassy when intelligence indicated that a suicidal terrorist attack was imminent.

In some cases, teams join the protective detail assigned to high-profile U.S. officials, especially the secretary of state. This extra safety measure is typically taken when the secretary needs to travel to a high-threat location, often in pursuit of an immediate diplomatic objective.

■ ■

Beyond Bodyguards

The motorcade moved fast—*very fast—through roads torn up by tanks and artillery shells. Nearly one dozen Chevy Suburbans tore past, crammed with guards wearing bulletproof Kevlar body armor, which was labeled with the words "DSS Federal Agent" in bright white lettering. Aiming M4 carbine rifles out of open rear doors, they monitored the rooftops and trees for signs of trouble, such as the glare of a sniper scope shimmering in*

A DSS agent is suited up and heavily armed in preparation for a protective mission.

the sun or a speeding car attempting to ram the convoy. The agents knew that terrorists in the area might be looking for a high-profile target, and few targets ranked higher than Secretary of State Colin Powell. But the procedure was clear and precise. Anything or anyone who threatened the secretary, no matter from which side of the two warring factions, would face a punishing wall of 5.56mm fire.

Powell was on his way to Ramallah, in the Palestinian-held West Bank, in May 2002. The trip was a last-ditch effort to convince Palestinian leader Yasser Arafat to renounce terrorism against Israel. The task would not be easy. The Palestinian-Israeli conflict had dragged on for more than fifty years, and it was as bitter and bloody as ever. Arafat, surrounded by Israeli troops, was eager to show the chief U.S. diplomat that he could not be intimidated. Meanwhile, Palestinian militants had declared a holy war against the United States for its support of Israel. Potential threats to Powell lurked around every unfamiliar corner.

Reaching Arafat's presidential compound, the motorcade passed columns of Israeli armor. It screeched to a halt as the agents emerged from their armored SUVs to assume defensive positions, surrounding Secretary Powell with a ring of counterterrorist firepower.

■ ■

| RESCUE FORCE | Another federal tool of U.S.

counterterrorism is the FBI and its Hostage Rescue Team (HRT). HRT is the primary national force tasked with responding to serious terrorist incidents in the mainland United States.

HRT's creation was spurred largely by fears of a large-scale terrorist attack during the 1984 Olympics in Los Angeles, California, and the unit became fully operational in September 1983. Based at the FBI's sprawling facility in Quantico, Virginia, HRT members traveled around

HRT trainees carry out a practice rescue at the FBI Training Academy in Quantico, Virginia.

the globe training with top counterterrorist teams, from Germany's GSG-9 to Britain's famed SAS. Back at Quantico, the HRT built what many experts consider one of the world's finest counterterrorism training facilities. Trained to respond to any hostage-taking incident in the United States, the team is believed to be able to deploy anywhere in the country within four to six hours of being notified. From the outset, negotiations were the team's first and primary strategy to respond to an attack. But should negotiations fail, the next step would be lethal and unforgiving force.

HRT is the primary unit to respond to aircraft hijackings. In its early years, the team was also sent overseas several times to oversee the capture and return of terrorists responsible for attacks against the United States. In September 1987, HRT seized Fawaz Younis, a Lebanese terrorist responsible for the hijacking and bombing of a Royal Jordanian jetliner and a participant in the hijacking of TWA Flight 847. Lured to a yacht traveling in international waters, Younis was arrested by HRT operatives lying in wait. HRT traveled to Pakistan in February 1995 to help the DSS transport the captured Ramzi Yousef to the United States. HRT members also went to Yemen to assist FBI investigators seeking evidence after the *Cole* bombing in 2000.

Following the September 11, 2001, attacks, HRT was immediately mobilized, and it has been part of numerous terrorist investigations in the United States ever since. Although many of these operations remain classified, HRT is believed to have investigated numerous targets thought to be al-Qaeda safe houses inside the United States.

| A NEW DEFENSE | Among the many changes caused by September 11 was the creation of an entirely new federal department to coordinate critical security information, to anticipate and prevent attacks, and to respond to threats. In November 2002, President George W. Bush officially created the Department of Homeland Security.

The mission of the Department of Homeland Security is to develop a national counterterrorism plan. One element of this task is to create a more unified approach. After September 11, many members of the intelligence community felt that inadequate communication and cooperation among existing agencies and

A DELICATE BALANCE

September 11 left Americans with deeply troubling questions about the effectiveness of U.S. counterterrorism. How could national intelligence have missed the planning of such a far-reaching and sophisticated attack? Could the attacks have been prevented? And how could another such tragedy be averted? The Department of Homeland Security arose in response to these questions.

However, while most U.S. citizens agreed that changes were needed, not all of the government's plans met with public approval. For example, the U.S.A. Patriot Act, introduced in October 2001, increased the government's power to track information and individuals within the United States. The act also introduced new crimes with new penalties. Many people feared that such sweeping reforms endangered their constitutional rights,

Demonstrators gather to protest the Patriot Act and its main defender, Attorney General John Ashcroft.

and citizens, businesses, and local governments have been outspoken in challenging the act.

Another controversial proposal was the Terrorism Information Awareness program, which would have given government agencies greater freedom to use surveillance and monitor citizens' activities. Concern about the measure's possible threat to privacy and personal freedom was widespread, and the program stalled in 2003. But as of mid-2003, the government still faces the challenge of protecting its citizens from terrorism without putting their rights at risk—a delicate balance that will clearly be difficult to achieve. ■

departments may have hindered counterterrorism efforts. To address those lapses, Homeland Security employees gather information from counterterrorism groups such as the military, the CIA, and the FBI. The creation of this new department has added yet another weapon to the federal counterterrorism arsenal.

LOCAL LAW ENFORCEMENT

Although they may be less fascinating than groups such as Delta, the nation's police officers are in fact frontline warriors in the fight against terrorism. The men and women of city, county, and state law enforcement are often the first to respond to a crisis. By working to protect their towns and cities on a day-to-day basis, they play an essential role in preventing terrorism. In the awful event of an attack, they also become the last line of defense.

Under Siege

The city is Los Angeles.
A downtown high-rise building has been seized by terrorists. Their demands are unclear, as are their intentions. Yet a few critical facts are as clear as gunshot: the terrorists are heavily armed, well trained, and prepared to die. The usual hustle and bustle of downtown Los Angeles is paralyzed by the attack. The morning traffic freezes as ambulances and fire trucks zigzag through the congested lanes. Dozens of

Los Angeles police officers take part in a rapid-fire counter-terrorism training scenario.

black-and-white patrol cars clog the street outside the seized building, while a helicopter from the department's elite Air Support Division hovers high above in an airborne patrol. The bomb squad truck arrives, and officers scramble to unload their gear.

Another team of officers reaches the scene and moves calmly through the police tape and the crowds. The team brings a mini-arsenal with it. One officer shoulders an M16 5.56mm assault rifle fitted with a laser sighting device, while another carries a Benelli automatic 12-gauge shotgun and several cases of electronic and communications gear. Snipers armed with high-powered guns head to nearby rooftops to assume firing positions. Several team members carry entry tools as they race up the stairs of the building, and every officer has a .45 automatic strapped to his hip. Ready to meet any threat, they know that they are the city's last resort. If terrorists strike a U.S. city, the citizens aren't going to phone the army or the FBI. They're going to dial 911.

■ ■

The scene above was a training exercise that pulled in all branches of Los Angeles's local law enforcement. In addition to patrol officers, most police departments field Special Weapons and Tactics units, or SWAT teams. Their mission is to confront the most dangerous situations.

Seattle police conduct an elaborate homeland security drill. Similar exercises around the country help prepare local forces to deal with terrorism.

Team members are uniquely equipped to handle incidents in which buildings have been seized, hostages taken, or other grave threats to human life have arisen. To counter such threats, these units are armed with heavy weapons, protective equipment, special deployment vehicles, and specialized training.

SWAT teams dedicate tremendous time and resources to the special training and instruction that allow them to handle out-of-the-ordinary situations. SWAT team officers, who have taken it upon themselves to be the first through the door on the most dangerous assignments, cannot afford to be underprepared. Some units—such as Los Angeles's SWAT platoon and the Miami-Dade Police Special Response Team—have even trained with U.S. military counterterrorist forces.

■ ■

Assault and Rescue

The officers lined up in two rows, called sticks. Hidden behind the building, they carried submachine guns, semiautomatic handguns, and heavy ballistic shields. When the order was given, they emerged from their staging area quickly and quietly, crouching as they ran toward the city bus baking in Miami's June heat. One stick of officers moved to the right side of the bus, training their weapons on the windows. The other stick moved toward the left. A sniper positioned atop a building about three hundred feet away fired one round, piercing the fortified glass of the city bus and dropping the head terrorist. The assault was under way.

The officers moved quickly and determinedly. Prying open the bus's main door, they stormed the crowded vehicle before the remaining terrorists could turn their guns on the panic-stricken hostages. "Get down!" the officers shouted as they raced up the aisle with weapons at the ready. Once the bus was secure, the officers got the hostages safely off the vehicle to identify them—and to identify possible terrorists posing as captives. The entire assault took less than ninety seconds, but it wasn't good enough. One of the training officers, wearing a sweat-soaked black T-shirt and fatigue trousers, looked at his watch, shook his head, and ordered the officers to do it again. "If you aren't going to get it right," the instructor shouted, "then you and the hostages will die!"

In the harsh midday Florida sun, SWAT officers from throughout Florida and beyond had assembled at the Miami-Dade Police Department Training Center. They were there to hone their skills in tubular assault—storming a small structure such as a plane, a train, or a bus. Their ultimate objective in such an assault was to subdue or eliminate the terrorists before they had a chance to execute the hostages. Roasting in their gear, the units toiled on in the Miami sun, spending hours perfecting skills that they hoped would never be needed on their streets.

■ ■

| THE STREETS OF NEW YORK | The largest police

tactical team in the United States is the New York City Police Department's Emergency Service Unit (ESU), which fields approximately four hundred officers. Under the command of the NYPD's Special Operations Division, ESU traces its creation to 1925, when a reserve force of volunteer officers was formed to handle extraordinary rescue assignments. Many of these officers were also part-time carpenters, welders, and electricians. With diverse backgrounds and knowledge of many kinds of equipment, they brought a wealth of skills and gear to the

ESU officers patrol New York City's Rockefeller Plaza. They are heavily armed and accompanied by a trained police dog.

READY TO ROLL

A small fleet of vehicles is on hand to respond to the many emergencies for which ESU officers are trained. Ranging from modified pickup trucks to million-dollar mobile workstations, the onboard equipment of these vehicles includes:

- Emergency and rescue gear, including scuba gear, inflatable raft with oars, binoculars, gas masks, helmets and shields, fire extinguishers and hoses, animal control kit, high-intensity lights, battering ram, and ladders
- First aid kit including resuscitator, burn kit, stretchers, blankets, and splints
- Nonlethal weapons such as stun guns, Mace and pepper spray, and handcuffs
- Heavy weapons including pump shotgun, Heckler and Koch MP5 9mm submachine gun, Ruger Mini-14 assault rifles, 9mm semiautomatic pistol, and 37mm tear gas launcher
- Tools such as bolt and wire cutters, lock buster, sledgehammer, jackhammer, axe, drill, crowbar, chain saw, lanterns, and flares

Other ESU vehicles include a bomb truck, units carrying mobile power generators, a decontamination trailer, a photo observation vehicle, and two snowmobiles. ■

modified fire trucks in which they rode. As time went on, the trucks came to carry more specialized emergency and lifesaving equipment, and all officers took emergency medical training. The ESU also boasted serious firepower. Its officers carried Thompson submachine guns, which gave the unit the daunting nickname of the Machine Gun Squad.

As time went on, the ESU also gained a counterterrorist and hostage-rescue role. As a major metropolis, New York City has long been a prime target for both domestic and international terrorist groups. As a result, the NYPD ESU has had more experience than any other U.S. law enforcement agency in dealing with terror. In 1993 ESU was the first unit to respond to the World Trade Center bombing. Unit members helped evacuate thousands of victims from the buildings, and ESU squads even swung down on ropes from NYPD helicopters to rescue trapped victims. The unit has also provided security and counterterrorist power for major figures visiting New York and at events taking place in the city.

| **TERROR FROM WITHIN** | The ESU, like other U.S. counterterrorist forces, is principally designed to prevent foreign terrorists from reaching or harming U.S. citizens. However, its officers have sometimes been forced to confront attacks from the inside, executed by U.S. terrorists and targeting other Americans. One such attack took place in Oklahoma City, Oklahoma, on April 19, 1995.

New York's streets were relatively quiet that day. Some of ESU's members were on patrol, while other crews monitored radio and television news back at headquarters. But the quiet was shattered when the first reports began rolling in around 10:04 A.M. A terrorist's bomb had ripped through Oklahoma City's Alfred P. Murrah Federal Building.

ESU sprang into action. It acted under a federal program called the Urban Search and Rescue Program. This system allowed on-call rescue force of ESU officers, firefighters, and EMTs to be sent anywhere in the United States on short notice. By 12:05 A.M. on April 20, ESU had convoyed the emergency unit to JFK International Airport. A U.S. Air Force C-141 then transported them and their gear to Oklahoma City to begin the search-and-rescue operation. In all, the force consisted of more than sixty members, including some twenty ESU officers. Although many of them had witnessed the World Trade Center bombing in 1993, nothing prepared them for the destruction they faced in Oklahoma.

Working twelve-hour shifts in the building's rubble-filled shell, the force executed a desperate but highly organized search. The officers were determined to find and rescue any wounded or trapped survivors from the chaos. They worked feverishly through the nights, sifting through mangled steel and fallen slabs of concrete. But there were few survivors to be found. The attack

ESU members joined the search-and-rescue mission following the Oklahoma City bombing.

had killed 168 people and had injured more than 500, making it the worst act of domestic terrorism in the United States until September 11.

The Oklahoma City bombing was carried out by Timothy McVeigh, a twenty-seven-year-old former soldier with a private agenda against the U.S. government. This attack by an isolated, fanatical man bore little resemblance to those strikes carried out by organized networks such as Hezbollah or al-Qaeda. Nevertheless, it was every bit as real and dangerous, and U.S. counterterrorist forces responded with the same dedication that they had brought to other crises.

| UNEXPECTED CHALLENGES | The ESU is unusual in its

diversity and flexibility. This range of skills came into use in Oklahoma City. It has also brought the unit into some unusual situations. For example, the ESU is one of the only U.S. law enforcement units to have directly confronted suicide bombers. One dramatic showdown took place on a steamy night in July 1997.

■ ■

Close Call

The sergeant signaled his team to move forward. The officers who huddled behind him clutched their weapons tightly, shoving aside the nagging thought that this was a suicide mission. They crept down the rat-infested hallway toward the apartment door. Once through that door, the officers knew quick action was their only chance. If the Palestinians heard them coming, they would—as threatened— detonate their bombs, blowing up the cops and everyone else in the building in a thunderous explosion. There could be no second guessing, no fear, and no hesitation.

Midnight was usually pretty quiet for the ESU crews. But on the night of July 31, 1997, the terrified roommate of two Palestinian men living in the Brooklyn neighborhood had come to the NYPD to reveal a murderous plot. The informant told investigators that his roommates were members of the Palestinian terrorist group Hamas. They intended, he said, to blow themselves up on a subway train heading to Manhattan. The attack was scheduled for the morning rush hour, when the subway car would be full. Morning was only a few hours away. There was no time to waste.

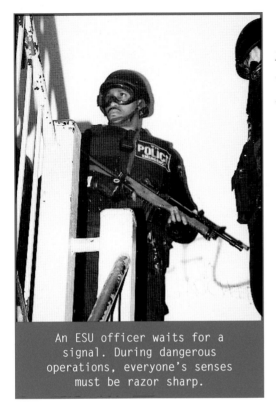

An ESU officer waits for a signal. During dangerous operations, everyone's senses must be razor sharp.

There was, however, plenty to worry about. The cops would have only a split second to assess the situation inside the apartment, make a decision, and fire if they saw a risk. But what if the informant was wrong—or lying—and the Palestinians were not building a bomb? Or what if they had other Hamas members with them? The unforeseeable risks seemed endless.

Steeling their nerves, the entry team stormed the apartment in a rush. The two Palestinians inside resisted, reaching for switches to detonate their explosives. But the ESU responded with lightning-quick reflexes, wounding the terrorists before they could proceed with their plot.

The flexibility and skills that allowed the ESU to succeed against suicide bombers also equips its officers to rescue people from collapsing buildings, plane crashes, automobile wrecks, and nearly every other imaginable disaster—including terrorism. When the first hijacked aircraft crashed into the north tower of the World Trade Center on the morning of September 11, ESU squads rushed to lower Manhattan to help spearhead citywide emergency rescue operations. Fourteen ESU officers were killed when the two towers came crashing down.

9/11

The officers prided themselves *on having done and seen it all in the ESU. They had raided crack houses and had rescued people from the most gruesome of accidents. But September 11 was more horrific than anything they had ever witnessed. The sight of people*

*throwing themselves out of windows on the towers' ninetieth floors
would be burned into their memories forever. And this was no
accident. It was a deliberate and cold-blooded terrorist attack on their
city, their nation, and their way of life.*

*Racing to their vehicles for their heavy weapons and protective
vests, the officers loaded up with oxygen packs to provide oxygen to
victims and prepared to enter the inferno. But this was far from an
ordinary fire. What if the terrorists had hijacked more planes? What if
they launched missiles or opened up with machine-gun fire? No matter
what, this mission was unlikely to be a simple rescue. Wearing the
heavy, suffocating protective gear would make climbing the stairs of the
World Trade Center difficult. The MP5 submachine guns and Mini-
14s they carried would be cumbersome when carrying people down the
stairs. But none of that mattered. The ESU officers rushed into the
towers knowing the consequences and knowing what had to be done.
Fourteen of the unit's officers lost their lives that day.*

■ ■

As the fight against terror continues, the ESU remains an
important part of the struggle. In addition, other local, county, and state
law enforcement groups also play a major role in protecting their people
from harm every day.

EPILOGUE*

The U.S. War on Terror is far from over. A number of important victories have been won, such as the CIA's August 2003 capture of Riduan Isamuddin, also known as Hambali. This al-Qaeda operative was believed to have been behind October 2002 bombings in Bali, Indonesia, that killed more than 180 people—most of them Westerners. He may also have played a role in an August 2003 bombing of a hotel in Jakarta, Indonesia, that killed 12. And in Iraq, U.S. counterterrorism enjoyed an enormous victory in December 2003 with the capture of Saddam Hussein. Hussein's arrest ended one of the largest manhunts in history. The capture also brought tentative hopes that anti-American violence in the region would decrease. However, attacks continue to plague U.S. troops serving on Iraq's unconventional postwar battleground.

Other important challenges also lie ahead. The Taliban is regrouping in Afghanistan and Pakistan in the hopes of regaining power. In addition, a videotape that surfaced in September 2003 showing bin Laden and his top aide, Ayman al-Zawahiri, suggested that al-Qaeda was still coordinating new attacks. These fears were strengthened by deadly bombings in Istanbul, Turkey, in November 2003 and Madrid, Spain, in March 2004. In both cases, the strikes were strongly suspected to be al-Qaeda's work, and arrested suspects were proven to have ties to the terrorist network. As international counterterrorist teams investigated the attacks, U.S. forces stood ready to cooperate and assist in the global fight against al-Qaeda.

Also as part of this effort, U.S. counterterrorist units, including Task Force 121, launched Operation Mountain Storm in March 2004. Thought to be working with Pakistani troops in the wild Pakistan-Afghanistan borderlands, U.S. forces intensified the hunt for bin Laden, other al-Qaeda operatives, and Taliban members. And while such operations proceed, U.S. military and intelligence groups will also continue to monitor ongoing threats in the coming months and years. ■

*Please note that the information contained in this book was current at the time of publication. To find sources for late-breaking news, please consult the websites listed on page 69.

TIMELINE

1775–1783 Early special forces are used during the American Revolution.

1916 The forerunner of the modern Diplomatic Security Service (DSS) is formed.

1925 An early version of New York's Emergency Service Unit (ESU) is formed.

1939 World War II begins.

1942 The Office of Strategic Services, forerunner of the Central Intelligence Agency (CIA), is formed.

1945 World War II ends. The Cold War begins.

1947 The CIA is formed.

1948 The State of Israel is founded. The Palestinian-Israeli conflict begins.

1961 President John F. Kennedy takes office and brings new focus to the need for special forces.

1962 The first Navy SEAL teams are formed.

1965 U.S. troops join the Vietnam War. Many special forces take part in the conflict.

1968 The Popular Front for the Liberation of Palestine hijacks an Israeli plane, bringing international attention to terrorism.

1970 Skyjack Sunday occurs. The Sontay raid fails.

1972 The Munich Olympic Massacre takes place.

1977 Delta Force is formed.

1979 The U.S. embassy in Tehran, Iran, is seized by Islamic militants. The Soviet Union invades Afghanistan.

1980s CIA agents assist the mujahideen in Afghanistan.

1980 Delta Force attempts to rescue the Iran hostages in Operation Eagle Claw. The operation fails, and eight U.S. servicepeople are killed.

1983   Terrorists bomb the U.S. embassy in Beirut, the U.S. Marine barracks in Beirut, and the U.S. embassy in Kuwait City, Kuwait. The Federal Bureau of Investigation's Hostage Rescue Team is created.

1984   CIA agent William Buckley is kidnapped in Beirut.

1985   Delta and SEAL operators respond to Hezbollah's TWA hijacking and to the *Achille Lauro* hijacking, but their efforts are thwarted by local governments. The modern DSS is formed.

1989   Delta carries out Operation Just Cause to rescue Kurt Muse from a Panamanian prison.

1993   ESU and other emergency forces respond to the bombing of the World Trade Center. Delta takes part in a failed mission to Somalia.

1995   The DSS helps capture al-Qaeda member Ramzi Yousef.

1997   The CIA updates its Special Operations Group (SOG). An ESU team apprehends Palestinian terrorists allegedly planning to bomb city subways.

1998   U.S. special forces respond to bombings of two U.S. embassies in Africa.

2000   The USS *Cole* is bombed in Yemen by agents believed to be members of al-Qaeda.

2001   The September 11 terrorist attacks strike New York, Washington, D.C., and Pennsylvania. U.S. special forces head to Afghanistan.

2002   A SOG drone kills five al-Qaeda members in Yemen. The Department of Homeland Security is created.

2003   CIA SOG agents capture al-Qaeda lieutenant Khalid Shaikh Mohammed in Pakistan. Task Force 121, along with other U.S. forces in Iraq, captures former Iraqi dictator Saddam Hussein.

2004   Abu Abbas dies in an Iraqi prison. U.S. counterterrorist forces launch Operation Mountain Storm in the border regions between Afghanistan and Pakistan, stepping up the search for bin Laden and other al-Qaeda leaders.

SELECTED BIBLIOGRAPHY

Baer, Robert. *See No Evil: The True Story of a Ground Soldier in the CIA's War on Terrorism.* New York: Crown Publishing, 2002.

Beckwith, Charles A., and Donald Knox. *Delta Force: The Army's Elite Counterterrorist Unit.* New York: Harcourt, 1983.

Bolger, Daniel P. *Americans at War, 1975–1986: An Era of Violent Peace.* Novato, CA: Presidio Press, 1988.

Carney, Colonel John. T., and Benjamin F. Schemmer. *No Room for Error: The Covert Operations of America's Special Tactics Units from Iran to Afghanistan.* New York: Ballantine Books, 2002.

Cooley, John K. *Payback: America's Long War in the Middle East.* Riverside, NJ: Brassey's, 1991.

Couch, Dick, and Cliff Hollenbeck. *The Warrior Elite: The Forging of Seal Class 228.* New York: Crown Publishing, 2001.

Coulson, Danny O., and Elaine Shannon. *No Heroes: Inside the FBI's Secret Counter-Terror Force.* New York: Pocket Books, 1999.

Durant, Michael J., and Steven Hartov. *In the Company of Heroes.* New York: Putnam Penguin, 2003.

Emerson, Steven. *Secret Warriors: Inside the Covert Military Operations of the Reagan Era.* New York: G. P. Putnam's Sons, 1988.

Haney, Eric L. *Inside Delta Force: The Story of America's Elite Counterterrorist Unit.* New York: Delacorte Press, 2002.

Katz, Samuel M. *Relentless Pursuit: The DSS and the Manhunt for the al-Qaeda Terrorists.* New York: Forge Books, 2002.

Kelly, Orr. *Brave Men, Dark Waters: The Untold Story of the Navy SEALs.* Novato, CA: Presidio Press, 1992.

Kessler, Ronald. *Inside the CIA: Revealing the Secrets of the World's Most Powerful Spy Agency.* New York: Pocket Books, 1994.

Kyle, James H. *The Guts to Try: The Untold Story of the Iran Hostage Rescue Mission by the On-Scene Desert Commander.* New York: Orion Books, 1990.

Marcinko, Richard, and John Weisman. *Rogue Warrior.* New York: Pocket Books, 1992.

Moore, Robin. *The Hunt for Bin Laden: Task Force Dagger.* New York: Random House, 2003.

Waller, Douglas C. *The Commandos: The Inside Story of America's Secret Soldiers.* New York: Simon and Schuster, 1994.

Walsh, Michael J., and Greg Walker. *SEAL!: From Vietnam's PHOENIX Program to Central America's Drug Wars: Twenty-six Years with a Special Operations Warrior.* New York: Pocket Books, 1996.

Whitcomb, Christopher. *Cold Zero: Inside the FBI Hostage Rescue Team.* New York: Warner Books, 2002.

FURTHER READING AND WEBSITES

Books

Burnett, Betty. *Delta Force: Counterterrorism Unit of the U.S. Army.* New York: Rosen Publishing Group, 2003.

Cothran, Helen, ed. *The Central Intelligence Agency.* San Diego: Greenhaven Press, 2003.

Goldstein, Margaret. *Iran in Pictures.* Minneapolis: Lerner Publications Company, 2004.

Gottfried, Ted. *Homeland Security versus Constitutional Rights.* Brookfield, CT: 21st Century Books, 2003.

Hopkins, Ellen. *U.S. Special Operations Forces.* Chicago: Heinemann Library, 2003.

Katz, Samuel M. *Jihad: Islamic Fundamentalist Terrorism.* Minneapolis: Lerner Publications Company, 2004.

Keeley, Jennifer. *Deterring and Investigating Attack: The Role of the FBI and the CIA.* San Diego: Lucent Books, 2004.

Marcovitz, Hal. *Terrorism.* Philadelphia: Chelsea House Publishers, 2001.

Stewart, Gail B. *America under Attack: September 11, 2001.* San Diego: Lucent Books, 2002.

Torr, James D. *Responding to Attack: Firefighters and Police.* San Diego: Lucent Books, 2004.

Woolf, Alex. *Osama bin Laden.* Minneapolis: Lerner Publications Company, 2004.

Young, Mitchell, ed. *The War on Terrorism.* San Diego: Greenhaven Press, 2003.

Websites

The Center for Defense Information: Terrorism Project
<http://www.cdi.org/terrorism>
This site provides detailed articles on homeland security, U.S. defenses against terrorism, and a variety of other topics related to terrorism.

Central Intelligence Agency: The War on Terrorism
<http://www.cia.gov/terrorism/index.html>
The CIA's website offers a wealth of articles and materials on U.S. counterterrorism.

Explore the Navy: U.S. Navy SEALs
<http://www.navy.com/jsp/explore/comunity/seals/index.jsp?cid=29&pid=2>
This official U.S. Navy site offers information on SEALs training, equipment, and recruitment.

Federal Bureau of Investigation: War on Terrorism
<http://www.fbi.gov/terrorinfo/counterrorism/waronterrorhome.htm>
The FBI's website provides information on most-wanted terrorists, the September 11 attacks, and much more.

Special Operations.com
<http://www.specialoperations.com/Counterterrorism/default.html>
Find descriptions of a wide range of counterterrorism missions and raids at this site, as well as other information on special operations around the world.

Terrorism Questions and Answers
<http://www.terrorismanswers.com>
This site, operated by the Markle Foundation (a nonprofit group that studies communications and media), presents a wealth of information through question-and-answer sheets on various aspects of counterterrorism and terrorism.

U.S. Department of State
<http://www.state.gov>
This site, maintained by the U.S. government, provides a variety of links to information on terrorism and counterterrorism. Visit <http://www.state.gov/s/ct> for the Counterterrorism Office's site. Go to <http://www.state.gov/m/ds> for updates from the Bureau of Diplomatic Security and the DSS.

INDEX

ABOUT THE AUTHOR

Samuel M. Katz is an expert in the field of international terrorism and counterterrorism, military special operations, and law enforcement. He has written more than twenty books and dozens of articles on these subjects, as well as created documentaries and given lectures to a variety of law enforcement and counterterrorist agencies. Mr. Katz also serves as editor in chief of *Special Operations Report*, a magazine dedicated to the discussion of special operations around the world, and he has observed many U.S. and international counterterrorism units in action. The Terrorist Dossiers series is his first foray into the field of nonfiction for young people.

PHOTO ACKNOWLEDGMENTS

The images in this book were used with the permission of: © CORBIS, pp. 9, 38; © Reuters NewMedia Inc./CORBIS, pp. 10, 21, 27, 28, 41, 44; John F. Kennedy Library, p. 12; AP/Wide World Photos, pp. 13, 59; © Bettmann/CORBIS, pp. 14 (both), 15, 23, 42, 53; © Time Life Pictures/Getty Images, p. 16; © CORBIS SYGMA, p. 17; U.S. Navy Photo at Photri, p. 18; Defense Visual Information Center, pp. 19, 29; United States Air Force, pp. 24, 45; © Alain Nogues/CORBIS SYGMA, p. 25; U.S. Navy Photo, pp. 26, 31, 36 (both); © Leif Skoogfurs/CORBIS, p. 34; © J. Novak/Photri, p. 37; © Reza; Webistan/CORBIS, p. 40; © Patrick Robert/CORBIS, p. 43; © AFP/Getty Images, p. 47; © Markowitz Jeffrey/CORBIS SYGMA, p. 50; United States Department of Defense, p. 51; © Samuel M. Katz, pp. 52, 63; © Spencer Platt/Getty Images, p. 55; © Mendoza Tom/CORBIS SYGMA, p. 56; © Getty Images, p. 57; FEMA, p. 61. Cover: © AFP/Getty Images.